Exploring Space

A & C BLACK • LONDON

Exploring Space

contents

© Blake Publishing 2006
Additional material © A & C Black Publishers Ltd 2006

First published in Australia in 2006 by Blake Education Pty Ltd

This edition published in the United Kingdom in 2006 by
A & C Black Publishers Ltd, 38 Soho Square, London W1D 3HB
www.acblack.com

Hardback edition
ISBN-10: 0-7136-8382-1
ISBN-13: 978-0-7136-8382-0

Paperback edition
ISBN-10: 0-7136-8383-X
ISBN-13: 978-0-7136-8383-7

A CIP record for this book is available from the British Library.

Written by Maureen O'Keefe
Publisher: Katy Pike
Editor: Paul O'Beirne
Design and layout by The Modern Art Production Group

Photo credits: p9 (tr), p13 (tr, br), p18 (tl, br), p19 (tl, tr, bl), p20 (tr, mr), p21 (tl, tr, bl,
br), p22 (tr, mr), p23 (tl, tr, bl, br), p25 (tl, tr), p27 (tl) pictures courtesy NASA; p25
(br) (aap); p4 (br), p5 (top, br), p7 (top, bl), p11 (tl), p13 (tl, bl), p15 (tr, bl), p17 (tr),
p19 (br), p24 (tl, br), p25 (bl) (australian picture library); pp28–29 (Paul McEvoy)

Printed in China by WKT Company Ltd.

Exploring Space

Humans have explored space for thousands of years. In early times, they used their eyes to look at the heavens. The invention of the telescope allowed a deeper exploration of space. In more recent times, spacecraft and people have explored space.

Ancient civilisations studied the patterns of stars in the sky and observed the position of the Sun and the Moon. Early astronomers believed that the Sun, Moon and planets revolved around Earth. Nicolas Copernicus was the first astronomer to realise that Earth, other planets and moons revolved around the Sun. The invention of the telescope in the early 1600s allowed astronomers like Galileo Galilei to make discoveries about other planets and our solar system.

Probes, rockets and **satellites** are modern ways of exploring space. After the first unmanned spacecraft was launched successfully, people also went into space. Astronauts orbited the Earth and landed on its Moon. The next step was for longer stays in space aboard space shuttles and the International Space Station.

Now humans want to explore the furthest reaches of our solar system and the wider universe.

Before people ventured into space, scientists sent animals, so they could observe how the animals coped with being in space. The dog, Laika, was the first mammal from Earth to orbit the planet. Laika died from stress and overheating during her 1957 space mission in the Russian spacecraft Sputnik 2.

As telescopes have become more powerful, they have allowed us to observe planets, galaxies and **nebulae** in greater detail. In 1990 the Hubble telescope was sent into **orbit**.

GO FACT!

DID YOU KNOW?
Galileo discovered four moons orbiting Jupiter in January 1610.

5

Telescopes

Optical telescopes are used in observatories around the world. The optical telescopes in observatories are **reflecting telescopes**. Reflecting telescopes use mirrors to gather and focus light from distant objects.

Optical telescopes are built in high, dark places. The height reduces distortion caused by heat and Earth's atmosphere. Less distortion means that starlight entering the telescope is clearer. The telescope needs to be built in a dark place to reduce the interference from electric lights. Stars are much dimmer in the city because of the city lights.

How do optical telescopes work?

Light from a distant object enters the reflecting telescope through its open end. Light moves down to a large, curved mirror called the primary mirror. This collects the light and brings it to a point.

This light bounces off the primary mirror and heads towards a smaller mirror called the secondary mirror. This mirror reflects the image to an eyepiece on the side of the telescope.

The information sent to the eyepiece is stored on a computer. Astronomers use the computer to produce images of the object, and study these images, rather than looking through the eyepiece.

The Indian Astronomical Observatory, which sits 4517 metres above sea level, in Hanle, India, is the world's highest observatory telescope.

Amateur astronomers use **refracting telescopes**. The earliest telescopes were all refracting telescopes, including the famous and very simple telescope used by Galileo Galilei in the early 1600s.

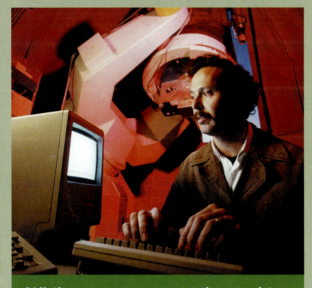

While astronomers study an object in space, the Earth is turning. A computer is used to control the movement of the telescope, so that it keeps pointing at the same object.

GO FACT!

WORLD'S LARGEST

The Keck telescopes, the world's largest optical telescopes, are located on the dormant Mauna Kea volcano on the island of Hawaii.

Hubble Telescope

The Hubble Space Telescope was launched into orbit in 1990. Astronomers can see further into space with Hubble than with any telescope on Earth.

The Hubble Space Telescope is a satellite which orbits Earth at a distance of about 600 kilometres (373 miles). It is a reflecting telescope and operates in a similar way to reflecting telescopes on Earth. It uses a large mirror to gather light from objects in space. The light bounces off the primary mirror and heads to a secondary mirror, which directs the light to equipment and high-**resolution** cameras on the Hubble telescope. This information is transmitted back to Earth.

The major difference between the Hubble telescope and ground-based telescopes is that Hubble is outside Earth's atmosphere. This allows astronomers to observe stars and planets more clearly, with less distortion. Hubble is also

clear of much of Earth's **gravity**, which 'bends' images.

Hubble can see 50 times further into space than the most powerful optical, ground-based telescope. It has 10 times better resolution and covers an area of space 350 times bigger than can be observed from Earth. This means Hubble can look beyond our solar system, find out how stars and galaxies form and locate planets orbiting other stars.

Hubble is the size of a large school bus. It fits inside the **cargo bay** of a space shuttle.

The Hubble Space Telescope spotted young brown dwarfs for the first time in the Orion Nebula. Brown dwarfs are so-called 'failed stars' because they are too small to be ordinary stars — they cannot sustain **nuclear fusion** in their cores the way our Sun does.

Hubble is serviced, and newer technology is installed, by astronauts on space walks. This means that Hubble can benefit from the same advances as ground-based telescopes.

GO FACT!

DID YOU KNOW?

The Hubble Space Telescope completes one full orbit of Earth every 97 minutes.

Rockets

Rockets **propel** spacecraft away from Earth's gravity and into space.

How does a rocket work?

Like all objects, rockets are held to Earth's surface by the pull of gravity. Rockets need to achieve a speed of 11 kilometres per second (7 miles per second), or 40 000 kilometres per hour (24 855 miles per hour) to escape Earth's gravity. Rockets have different sections, or stages, which help them to achieve this.

Two or three stages are stacked on top of each other to form the rocket. Each stage has its own engines and separate tanks of liquid fuel and liquid oxygen. The liquid fuel and liquid oxygen are pumped into a **combustion chamber** within the engine where they mix and burn. Hot gases are produced and rush backwards out of the engine. The escape of these gases propels the rocket forward.

The stages burn their fuel one after the other. Once the fuel in a stage has been used, the stage falls away from the rest of the rocket. The rest of the rocket has less weight to carry into space.

A three-stage rocket, Saturn V, was used to take astronauts to the Moon in the Apollo spacecraft. Stage 1 burnt its fuel over 2 minutes and 30 seconds, then separated from the rest of the rocket and fell back to Earth. Stage 2 then fired and lifted the astronauts into space. It too fell away. Finally, Stage 3 fired for 2 minutes and 30 seconds and sent Apollo into orbit around Earth. Stage 3 fired again for over five minutes to send Apollo towards the Moon. It then fell away from the spacecraft.

All spacecraft and satellites are taken into space by rockets.

GO FACT!

MOST POWERFUL

The largest and most powerful rocket ever built was the Saturn V rocket.

11

Probes

A space probe is a robot that carries scientific instruments. Probes fly past, orbit or land on a planet. Probes have explored planets and other bodies in our solar system since 1959.

The first space probes, the Soviet-made Luna probes, travelled to the Moon. In the 1960s, both the former **Soviet Union** and the United States sent probes to Venus. Although the **atmospheric pressure** and extreme heat caused many probes to fail, some did send information back to Earth. The Mariner 9 probe orbited Mars in 1971.

At the end of 1973, the Mariner 10 probe was launched. It flew past Venus on its way to Mercury. It did three **flybys** of Mercury during 1974 and 1975. The probe's images showed us that Mercury's surface is covered in craters.

Two Viking probes travelled to Mars in the mid-1970s. Each probe was made up of an **orbiter** and a **lander**. The orbiter released a lander craft that parachuted to the surface of Mars. The landers analysed the Martian soil samples and transmitted the information back to Earth.

Probes have studied other objects in the solar system. The Giotto probe, launched in 1985, flew close to Halley's Comet in 1986. Before the probe was damaged by dust from the comet, it transmitted data about the dust, gas and ice within the comet.

The Mariner probes were designed to investigate Mars, Venus and Mercury. In 1962, Mariner 2 became the first spacecraft to fly by another planet when it passed Venus.

The Viking landers conducted experiments on Martian soil to see if any form of life existed. Decades later, scientists are still arguing over the results.

GO FACT!

FIRST MOON LANDING

In 1959, the Soviet Luna 2 mission successfully crashed into the Moon. It made history by being the first man-made object to reach another world.

The Halley Multicolor Camera on the Giotto probe was destroyed when it veered too close to the tail of Halley's Comet. Before it was shattered, it took some spectacular pictures of the comet's nucleus.

Satellites

Satellites collect and transmit information as they orbit Earth.

How do satellites work?

A satellite is launched to a specific altitude. This position is maintained by Earth's gravity. Gravity pulls the satellite down just enough to keep the satellite travelling in a circular orbit, instead of flying away into space.

The body or frame of a satellite is made of metal, or a combination of materials, and is called the bus. The different parts of the satellite are attached to this frame. The bus provides protection during the launch and when the satellite is in orbit.

The Sun provides the satellite with power. **Arrays** of solar cells on the satellite convert sunlight into electrical energy, which provides power to rechargeable batteries on the satellite. The batteries store power for times when the Sun is not visible.

Nearly all satellites have a radio transmitter/receiver and an antenna. This allows them to transmit, or 'downlink' data to command centres on Earth. It also means that command centres can send or 'uplink' messages to the satellite. These command centres request information from the satellite, send adjustments to its course and can reprogram the instruments on the satellite.

Communications industries, such as Internet, TV and telephones, use satellites to transmit information quickly.

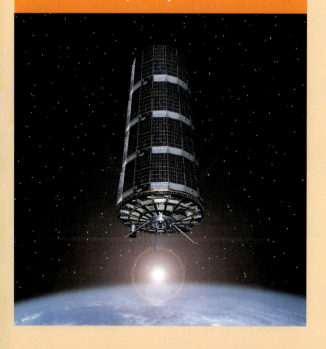

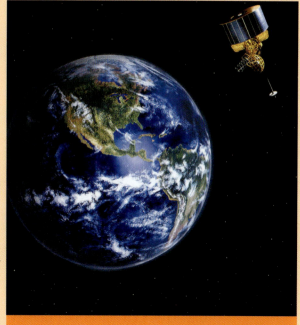

Satellites also have an Attitude Control System, which keeps the satellite pointing in the right direction.

The Soviet Union was the first country to launch a satellite. The Soviets launched Sputnik 1 on 4th October 1957. This was to be the beginning of the **space race** between the Soviet Union and the USA.

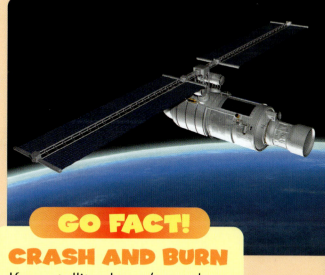

GO FACT!

CRASH AND BURN

If a satellite doesn't reach a suitable altitude, it can be affected by the **drag** of Earth's atmosphere and fall back into the atmosphere where it burns up.

15

Types of Satellite

Satellites provide information for weather forecasts and navigation, **monitor** conditions on Earth and transmit communication signals.

Weather satellites monitor climate patterns on Earth. They provide advance warnings of dangerous weather systems, such as cyclones. Some weather satellites are in geostationary orbits, which means they remain positioned over the same spot on Earth.

Communication satellites are also in geostationary orbits. These satellites receive television, data and telephone signals from one spot on Earth and re-transmit them to other places on Earth.

Navigation satellites can locate people's position and speed of movement on Earth. This system of navigation is called the Global Positioning System (GPS). GPS satellites continually transmit to receivers on Earth. Receivers may be on ships or planes, in motor vehicles, or carried by people. A receiver uses the signals from four satellites to calculate position, speed and exact time. These signals can also be tracked by search and rescue teams.

Scientific and observation satellites monitor conditions on Earth. Observation satellites fly at a lower orbit and take high-resolution images of the Earth's surface. These are used for mapping, and to record ice movements, crop problems and rainforest logging. Scientific satellites monitor volcanoes and changes in Earth's atmosphere.

Rockets launch satellites into space. On reaching orbit the satellites are released. Satellites travel at a speed of about 28 800 km/h (17 825 mph), which allows them to fly in an **arc** around Earth.

The Nimbus 7 weather satellite confirmed that an **ozone hole** exists over Antarctica.

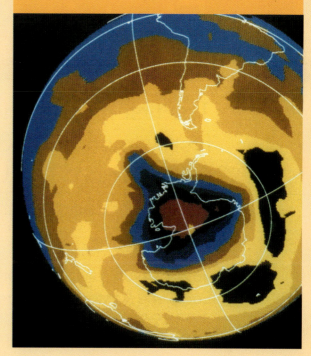

In the future, navigation satellites may assist in air traffic control.

HOW MANY?

There are over 8000 artificial objects orbiting Earth – 2500 of these are satellites.

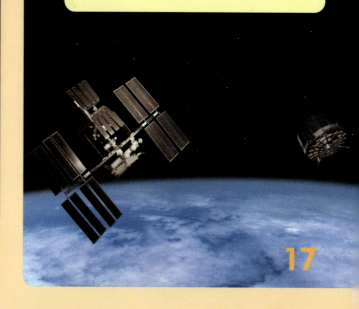

17

First in Space

The first man flew into space in 1961, and the first woman in 1963. Both were from the former Soviet Union. The United States space program concentrated on landing on the Moon.

Yuri Gagarin, a pilot in the Soviet Union's Air Force, orbited Earth in a Vostock spacecraft in April 1961. The flight took less than two hours. To return to Earth, Gagarin ejected from the spacecraft at 7000 metres and parachuted to the ground. The spacecraft used another parachute to land. In 1963, Valentina Tereshkova orbited Earth 48 times in Vostok 6 and spent almost three days in space.

In February 1962, John Glenn, in Friendship 7, became the first US astronaut to orbit Earth. The US Apollo program was devoted to the goal of landing a man on the Moon and returning him safely to Earth. In December 1968 Apollo 8 orbited the Moon with three crew members on board. The crew of Apollo 9 took part in the first flight of the **lunar module**. In May 1969, Apollo 10 carried out the final practice for a moon landing. It travelled to within 15 km (9.3 miles) of the Moon's surface and made the first live, colour TV broadcast from space.

Valentina Tereshkova, the first woman to venture into space, spent 2 days, 22 hours and 50 minutes in space. While orbiting Earth in Vostok 6, she took photographs of Earth's atmosphere. These photographs were later used by scientists to identify the different layers within the atmosphere.

Moon rock weighing 381.7 kg was brought back to Earth by the Apollo program. Most of the material is stored at the Lunar Receiving Laboratory in **Houston**, Texas, USA.

There were 11 manned flights in the Apollo program – Apollo 7 to Apollo 17. Apollo 4 to Apollo 6 were unmanned test flights (officially there was no Apollo 2 or Apollo 3).

GO FACT!

DANGEROUS
In January 1967, the crew of Apollo 1 died during a simulated countdown on the launch pad. A fire killed three astronauts. As a result all further Apollo flights were unmanned until Apollo 7 in 1968.

19

The Moon Landing

Apollo 11 was the first manned spacecraft to land on the Moon.

Apollo 11 was launched on 16th July 1969. It had two separable modules. On board were three astronauts – Commander Neil Armstrong, Lunar Module pilot, Buzz Aldrin Jr. and Command and Service Module (CSM) pilot, Michael Collins.

The spacecraft took three days to reach the Moon's orbit. The next day, July 20th, Armstrong and Aldrin moved into the Lunar Module, named Eagle. Eagle and the CSM separated. Eagle descended to the Moon's surface. Armstrong radioed to the command centre on Earth:

"Houston, Tranquility Base here – the Eagle has landed."

A few hours later, Armstrong stepped onto the Moon's surface, saying:

"That's one small step for man, one giant leap for mankind."

Aldrin stepped onto the Moon 19 minutes later.

Almost 24 hours later, the two astronauts returned to the CSM in the Eagle. The CSM set its course for Earth on July 22nd.

Before entering Earth's atmosphere, the Command Module separated from the Service Module. Parachutes opened on the module to slow it down before it splashed into the Pacific Ocean on July 24th, 1969 The astronauts were picked up by the recovery ship, USS Hornet

The Apollo 11 astronauts raised the United States flag on the Moon. They had to insert wire along the top of the flag to hold it out because there is no wind on the Moon. The flag is still there.

On returning to Earth the mission wasn't quite finished for the three astronauts. They were **quarantined** for three weeks to ensure they hadn't caught anything on the Moon!

Armstrong and Aldrin spent 21 hours on the Moon, collecting rocks and soil, taking photographs and doing experiments. Meanwhile, the third astronaut, Collins, orbited the Moon in the CSM.

GO FACT!

DID YOU KNOW?

Attached to the landing pods of the Eagle were lunar-surface, sensing probes. Upon contact with the lunar surface, the probes sent a signal to the crew to shut down the descent engine.

21

Space Shuttles

Space shuttles are reusable spacecraft. They lift off from the launch pad like a rocket and return to Earth by gliding and landing on a runway. They have taken astronauts into space since 1981.

Design

A shuttle is also known as an orbiter. It is attached to an external fuel tank and two rocket boosters. At launch, the shuttle's three engines and the two rocket boosters provide power. After two minutes, the boosters fall away into the ocean and are collected by ships to be used again. After another six minutes, the fuel tank is empty and this too falls away. It is the only part which is not reusable.

Crew

The shuttle can carry up to seven crew members. Each mission has a commander, pilot, mission specialists and payload specialists. Mission specialists conduct experiments and conduct spacewalks. Payload specialists are people who are skilled at using the payload or cargo that is carried on the shuttle.

Uses

The shuttle can orbit Earth for up to 14 days. The shuttle also takes astronauts to and from the International Space Station. The shuttle docks with the station and astronauts use both areas to live and work. Shuttle astronauts carry out experiments on plants or crystals, test equipment and monitor the effects of living in space on the human body.

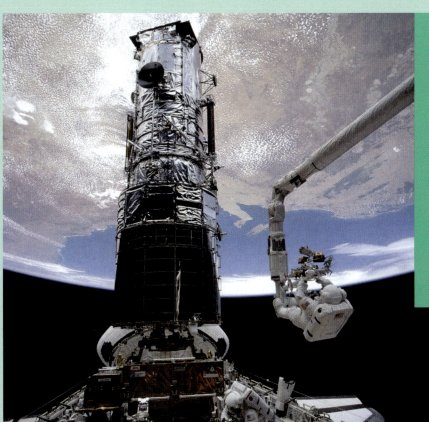

One famous repair mission occurred in 1993. Two astronauts captured the Hubble Space Telescope using a robotic arm to bring it into the cargo bay. During 35 hours of spacewalks they repaired a faulty lens and checked other instruments.

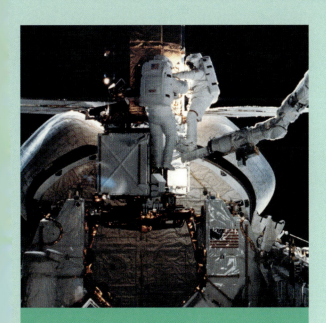

Sometimes the shuttle launches a new satellite from the cargo bay. Astronauts can also go on spacewalks to retrieve and repair satellites.

GO FACT!
DID YOU KNOW?
When landing, the shuttle uses a parachute to slow it down on the runway.

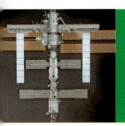

International Space Station

Space stations allow people to live in space for long periods of time. Supporters believe that space exploration benefits people on Earth. Other people are worried about the cost of a space station and whether the discoveries are worthwhile.

The International Space Station (ISS) will be the biggest structure ever built in space. Due to its size, people can live and work on the ISS for much longer than ever before. This allows scientists to gather information about the effects of living in space for long periods. This information could be helpful in working through the challenges of travelling to Mars.

Astronauts on the ISS conduct experiments in an environment where there is very little gravity. They can compare these results with what happens on Earth, where gravity affects everything. It increases our knowledge about why things behave the way they do.

Some scientists question whether the small number of crew on the ISS can devote enough time to conducting serious experiments. They say there is a limit to the resources on a space laboratory, which reduces the number and usefulness of experiments.

It is estimated that the cost from the start of the project to its completion in 2010 will be over $170 billion (£90 billion). Critics argue that this money could be better spent on Earth.

The first part of the ISS was launched in 1998. It won't be complete until at least 2010.

Having astronauts living on the ISS will provide data which can be used to further space exploration.

When the ISS is complete, it will be the size of a football stadium – 109 metres across and 80 metres long.

GO FACT!

INTERNATIONAL

Sixteen countries are building the ISS – USA, Russia, Canada, Japan, Brazil and the 11 countries of the European Space Agency.

Light Years Away

Distances in space are measured in light years. This is the distance that light travels in one year.

How do light years measure distance?

A light year is a measure of distance. A ray of light travels 9.5 trillion kilometres (6 trillion miles) in one year, or 9.5 million million kilometres. So a light year is 9 500 000 000 000 km.

Scientists use light years to measure distances in the universe because the universe is so immense. They use light years to measure distances between galaxies and between stars.

Light years also tell how long the light has taken to reach Earth. Alpha Centauri is one of the closest stars to Earth. It is 4.3 light years from Earth. This means that the light from this star has taken 4.3 years to reach Earth. We see the star as it was 4.3 years ago.

Our Sun is 150 million kilometres (93 million miles) from Earth. Light from the Sun takes eight minutes to reach us. This means that the Sun is eight light minutes away from Earth, and the light we see from the Sun is eight minutes old. We see the Sun as it was eight minutes ago.

Galaxies can extend from a few thousand to a million light years in **diameter**. Our Milky Way galaxy is 150 000 light years across.

In September 2004 the most distant space probe, Voyager 1, was 13 light hours (14.3 billion km or 8.9 billion miles) away from Earth. It took Voyager 27 years to cover that distance.

Nothing can move faster than light — no object, no matter, no information can directly overtake or catch up with light.

Making a Refracting Telescope

A refracting telescope uses two magnifying glasses to bend light and bring it into focus. For this to work, you need to find the length between two lenses that brings the image into focus. This is called finding the focal length.

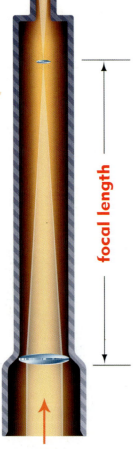

eye

focal length

light

You will need:

- a long cardboard tube
- 1 magnifying glass, about 1 cm diameter
- 1 magnifying glass, about 3 cm diameter
- scissors
- sticky tape
- a ruler
- a book with writing

1 Hold the smaller magnifying glass over the writing. Put the larger magnifying glass between the smaller glass and your eye.

2 Move the larger magnifying glass closer to you or further away until writing is in focus. The print will be upside down.

3 Use your newly discovered focal length to tape both magnifying glasses inside the cardboard tube.

4 Look at the night sky with your refracting telescope.

29

Early Space Exploration

Year	Spacecraft name	Details
1957	Sputnik 1	The Soviet Union launched the first man-made object to orbit the Earth. It orbited the Earth until January 1958.
1957	Sputnik 2	The Soviet Union launched the first mammal into space. The dog, Laika, orbited the Earth for seven days.
1958	Explorer 1	The first US satellite to orbit the Earth. On board was a scientific experiment by James A. Van Allen, which discovered Earth's **radiation belt**.
1959	Luna 1	The first satellite to orbit the Sun was launched by the Soviet Union.
1960	Tiros 1	The first successful weather satellite was launched by the US.
1961	Vostok 1	Vostok 1 was launched by the Soviet Union carrying Cosmonaut Yuri A. Gargarin, the first man in space. He orbited the Earth once.
1961	Freedom 7	Alan B. Shepard, the first US man in space, was aboard. Shepard became the first astronaut to return to Earth with his ship, because the Russian cosmonauts had to parachute away from theirs during landing.
1963	Vostok 6	Vostok 6 carried Soviet Cosmonaut Valentia Tereshkova, the first woman in space. She orbited the Earth 48 times.
1965	Voskhod 2	The first spacewalk was made from Soviet Voskhod 2 by Cosmonaut Alexei A. Leonov. The spacewalk lasted for 12 minutes.
1965	Venus 3	The Soviet Union launched Venus 3, the first man-made object to crash into the planet Venus on 1st March 1966.
1967	Soyuz 1	Soyuz 1 was launched, carrying Vladimir M. Komarov. On April 24th it crashed, killing Komarov. This was the first space-flight fatality.
1969	Apollo 11	Neil Armstrong and Edwin Aldrin, Jr. made the first manned landing on the Moon and took the first moon walk.

Glossary

arc part of the circumference of a circle

array a group of items arranged in rows and columns

atmospheric pressure the weight of the atmosphere pressing down on the Earth's surface

cargo bay a compartment in a space shuttle used during take off for storing devices such as satellites

combustion chamber the part of a cylinder where the explosion of the air-fuel mixture takes place

diameter the longest distance from one side of an object to the other, passing through the centre

drag resistance that slows an object down

flyby a flight at a low altitude over a planet

gravity the force that attracts all bodies in the Universe to each other

Houston the largest city in the state of Texas, USA; where NASA is based

lander a space vehicle that is designed to land on another planet

lunar module the section of the Apollo spacecraft designed to land on the Moon

monitor to record an activity or process

nebulae clouds of gas and dust in space

nuclear fusion two atoms coming together, giving off huge amounts of energy

optical telescope an astronomical telescope designed to collect and record light from cosmic sources

orbit the path that an object makes around another object, whilst under the influence of gravity

orbiter a spacecraft whose purpose is to orbit around a planet

ozone a form of oxygen, usually found in the stratosphere, and responsible for filtering out much of the Sun's ultraviolet radiation

ozone hole a hole in the protective layer of ozone in the upper atmosphere

probe an unmanned spacecraft which collects information about objects in space and sends it back to scientists on Earth

propel to push or drive forward

quarantine the isolation of people or animals for a period of time to ensure they don't spread disease

radiation belt a region of charged particles trapped in the Earth's magnetic field

reflecting telescope a telescope which uses a mirror to gather and focus light from a distant object

refracting telescope a telescope which uses a lens to gather and focus light from a distant object

resolution the sharpness or clarity of an image

satellite device that orbits the Earth and can be used for monitoring the weather, communications, etc.

Soviet Union a former communist country in eastern Europe and northern Asia; established in 1922; included Russia and 14 other republics; this group has split up and no longer exists.

space race battle between the United States and the Soviet Union for dominance in space exploration

Index